HOW TO WRITE A BOOK

HOW TO WRITE A BOOK

From Blank Page to Bookshelf

BILL VINCENT

RWG Publishing

CONTENTS

1	Publishing Links to help you with your books	1
2	Introduction to the Writing Process	2
3	Pre-Writing Phase	5
4	Crafting a Compelling Plot	7
5	Creating Dynamic Settings	9
6	The Art of Dialogue	11
7	Structuring Your Book	13
8	The Writing Process	15
9	Editing and Revising	17
10	Seeking Feedback	20
11	Preparing for Publication	22
12	Marketing and Promoting Your Book	25
13	Navigating the Publishing Industry	28
14	Self-Publishing vs. Traditional Publishing	30
15	Legal and Copyright Considerations	32
16	Building a Writing Routine	34

17	Balancing Writing with Other Commitments	36
18	Staying Motivated and Focused	38
19	The Importance of Community	40
20	Celebrating Milestones	43
21	Overcoming Rejection and Criticism	46
22	The Writer's Mindset	49
23	Writing Across Genres	51
24	The Future of Publishing	54
25	Conclusion and Final Thoughts	58
26	Publishing Links to help you with your books	60

Copyright © 2024 by Bill Vincent

All rights reserved. No part of this book may be reproduced in any manner whatsoever without written permission except in the case of brief quotations embodied in critical articles and reviews.

First Printing, 2024

CHAPTER 1

Publishing Links to help you with your books

Here are some great options for creating fantastic covers:
Economy Covers: https://tinyurl.com/5mhubyby
Premium Covers: https://tinyurl.com/yt3daf87
Here are some great options for Book Editing:
Premium: https://shorturl.at/tqdAz
Here are some great options for Book formatting:
Economy: https://shorturl.at/jNvsu
Here is a great master your audiobook to acx and audible requirements
https://tinyurl.com/ye2xkmna

CHAPTER 2

Introduction to the Writing Process

But why even write? If you're an average person, you'll write your entire life. However, you may not write a letter or a blog post every day; you may not even send a text message to friends often. But you will write. Whether it is a grocery list, a resume, a Christmas letter to family and friends, an article, or a book... you write. If you are in contact with other people at all, writing will be a part of your life. Even as a child, you wrote - letters to Santa, telling notes to your folks, school essays, and more. As writing is such a part of our lives, embrace it and share your thoughts with others. And if you have something unique to say or offer, write a book. After all, you may be the next person who visits a book club, is an interview guest on radio or TV, has a book signing, starts a national presentation tour, or simply helps other people with your advice.

Have you ever been inspired to write a book but you weren't sure where to begin? Perhaps you started writing but then you stopped and started, stopped and started. And then life took over and soon you've forgotten about your book. If you want to share your work with others, you have to first write down your thoughts. And then the editing process begins. In "How to Write a Book: From Blank Page to Bookshelf," I'll help guide you through the process even experienced authors continue to follow for publication.

1.1. Understanding the Creative Process

4) Incubation: This emptiness will go on forever, I know something is not quite right but I don't know quite what it is, I'm a part of it. Aim: to trust in the process of emptiness, to support subconscious problem solving and the arrival of new questions, to make new connections between old ideas.

3) Digestion. End of term feeling, you've been Arguing With Yourself (see task 4.1), discovering that you've been so busy writing you're too busy to read, everything is set in concrete and I might as well have been meant to be a productive worker. Aim: to trust in the process of reflection, contemplation, and stillness, to seed or check the material you are creating.

2) Focused creative effort. Everything fits together, it all makes sense, I'm lost in my task – at work, at play, I feel privileged to have access to my talents, it tastes like wine. Aim: to support the process of making the most of distinct creative skills.

The Creative Process: 1) Gathering. When your inspiration is at low ebb, and you may not even know what you are drawn to at the moment, gather experiences. Your mind is feeling cluttered, random bits of input are trying to find a use, you may be at a crossroads, and may be sorting things out. You may experience others as charismatic, since it appears that they know exactly what they want. Aim: to trust in the process of random, serendipitous experience.

By understanding the four fundamentally different stages of the creative process, you can be more effective in your book writing. We may feel differently about the output depending on the stage we are at, so it's useful to acknowledge that all stages are necessary, and to assign different tasks to different states of the process.

CHAPTER 3

Pre-Writing Phase

Writers who are intimidated by the daunting prospect of, "How do I get started?" will find that they are not alone. Voicing this concern is quite common among those who embark into the tracing of the written word for the first time, as well as, for those who are in the process of writing an or the next book. First and foremost, grab a piece of paper, open an electronic document or grab a writing implement. Write! At least, by writing, the first step will be drawn. Do not eliminate words, sentences, paragraphs or chapters because a writer has yet to start or complete them. By following this procedure, a written map is drawn—a map that designates the areas to be explored, to be expounded upon in greater detail, and to allow creative freedom to be expressed—to be expressed in a non-stop manner. If this procedure is not followed, the writer will experience writer's block and the finished result will hardly resemble anything near to a present in the form of a written work. Keep writing—writing, and writing—until the story comes to a natural conclusion.

Preparation is a must for those aspiring to write a book because writing a book is like running a marathon; it requires good or a certain level of physical and mental health. Like a marathon, it cannot be accomplished overnight. It requires numerous, tiresome days and months to complete. It took me five years to finish my first book! To succeed, aspiring writers should utilize their many skills and writing craft knowledge. At the end of the day, the written creativity is fashioned with punctuation marks, space between paragraphs, the pronoun "I" as uppercase, and how to properly capitalize words. It is the dictionary and thesaurus that a writer's mind rushed to in search of the desired word that satisfies the writer's need; not in just enunciating a particular word but a word that paints a mental image in the reader's mind. It is really the dictionary that is preferred.

2.1. Finding Inspiration

Each of us has experienced creative insight and intuition. We jokingly call it our "sixth sense." It is the ability to receive unexpected epiphanies that come from a deeper level than the one that usually remains uncovered as we go about our daily business—whether that is practicing law, fixing a leaky faucet, gardening, or writing a story. The choices we make at these unexpected intersections of insight can lead to the creative results a writer seeks: an insight that provides direction for a road not taken earlier in a story, a clear pattern in a plot, or a better understanding of our characters. First, we must be open to inspiration.

To become inspired, we must first believe that we possess the freedom to choose from an infinitely large pool of ideas located in the depths of our unique creative minds. Given certain stimuli like silence, beauty, and wonder, and certain conditions like inner peace, patience, and solitude, insight will flow. Ideas emerge out of nowhere or out of everyday possibilities that find their roots in our daily routines, chores, and moments of reflection. It is like a breeze of fresh air whisking through the windows of our homes and into our senses when we least expect it.

CHAPTER 4

Crafting a Compelling Plot

It's okay to enjoy the planning phase of writing and not be an organic writer—that's what this part of the book focuses on, after all. Even if you've never written a lick of fiction before, you know what a basic plot looks and feels like. There are a number of plots out there—detailed below in Crafting a Plot. The plot can be simple—an adventure during which the protagonist changes, or more complicated with more elements fitted in, multiple POV and subplots, and so on. If you're the type of writer who relishes a good free-write and pansies down the lane of story creation, this section does not have to be what you start with. Instead, it can be your lifeboat once you've written yourself off a metaphorical waterfall and need to bandage yourself up and make a better, more meaningful adventure for reader and characters.

In a book, the plot is what happens. Another way of thinking about it is the story's backbone. A reader is going to be lost and not care about your book if they can't find the plot. You need to be able to track your plot, to know where it's going, how the characters move—and more than that, you need to craft a compelling and exciting plot to begin with. That can seem incredibly daunting. After all, who wants to spend time creating a gripping plot and meticulously crafting it, only to have a reader not care about it? Not I! And hopefully neither you.

3.1. Developing Characters

Without that depth of feeling, usually a pleasure that we cared to repeat, we lose interest. Without the people, or thoughts, or experiences being vivid in our memories, we could not be proud of the fact that we could read and understand. All this has something to do with attention, and the writer's techniques for controlling his reader's attention. These matters will affect the flow of your book, the order of presentation. If you organize your book in the most interesting way, your readers will be glad, with a satisfaction that they barely understand, because your finished product will be something to remember.

Development of the main character can be the plot that carries a book. A book could be about a person. It could be a biography, a real story. Or it could be fiction, a tale, a parable, a recollection, or a rumination. No matter. If you choose that your book be about a person, the key to a successful book will be your ability to present this person and the other characters in a way that makes them vivid for the reader. There must be something about a person that involves us.

CHAPTER 5

Creating Dynamic Settings

Great settings are woven into the fabric of a story, like characters and plot. Descriptive phrases and words contribute to setting, as does imagery and literary devices such as simile and metaphor, creating sensory subtext that allows readers to draw conclusions. But the job of a setting is not to only give readers a picture to see. It must do more than that. The setting must tie into defining moments in the story and from there fill in some of the details of your characters and the direction of your story. The best settings present contrasts or elements that benefit your story. Such a world is an ironic, vivid, and memorable setting you return to use time and time again throughout your book. Such a world evolves from your everyday world.

To write good stories and create deeply moving experiences, writers need to understand the importance of setting and what it does for readers. By setting the scene, you give life to a picture for readers to see, which allows them to live vicariously through your written experiences. The more inviting and real the setting, the more compelling and dynamic your story becomes. This chapter delves into what is involved in creating different time-period settings by incorporating words that evoke the sounds, feel, and sights of a location in order to layer an aura onto the page. It is this aura that creates deep, evocative settings that draw readers in and hold their interest. Changes in setting can develop, enhance, and layer your plot and create visual subtext by suggesting things to readers at a subconscious level.

4.1. World-Building Techniques

The idea behind a world-building ten things list is to give you some important information about the nature of your world upfront, so that as you write, if the characters and their world are beginning to merge into a plot of their own, you can stop the chaos and either reassert the world details you know or change the nature of your characters' world to fit the way you are instinctively writing it. This list is particularly useful in the build-up to writing your first draft, as knowing enough about your world to know how things happen there will save you from the horrid common habits of hand-waving and info dumping within the work.

A popular and fun approach to world building is to write out a "Ten Things I Know About the World in My Story" sheet. This sheet is an at-a-glance guide to your world. It covers all the interesting and important things about it, from currency, political systems, and usable technology, up to and including what the inhabitants of your world eat for breakfast and how they get it. While this list can be written in note form, some writers would always advise that whichever approach you take to world-building, you should still use your notepad as well, as the combinations of written and visual ideas can lead to fantastic unique worlds that leap effortlessly off the page and into the reader's imagination.

CHAPTER 6

The Art of Dialogue

I always write the dialogue first, which is like a piece of music. Probably akin to the way my shock of hair requires pinning up. My drama training continues to stand me in good stead. Useless facts related to this are that only 7 per cent of the message is in the words, 38 per cent through the voice, and 55 per cent via body language. I keep listening for the asides, the natural triangulation between third party and the two in chat, and marvel at how first drafts can show an equilibrium that is basically what the characters feel and do throughout. The exploration of words is a major reason why I write. 'You get it right when you get it out' prevails throughout. Farewell then, to control and trust in subconscious order.

Talking heads. Hissing and spitting. What's the point of dialogue? Many characters like to run on. Should writers chop them off or find a way of making them shut up elegantly? Perhaps the discussion can be encapsulated in landscapes that help the dialogue rather than yawn and say, 'Window dressing'. Alternatively, a close study of David Mamet's plays and scripts might be in order. Pared down to the bone, his characters seldom talk more than 20 seconds before they are interrupted.

5.1. Writing Realistic Conversations

Some people aren't comfortable in any situations where dialogue could be helpful; they feel like they're in a hierarchy and want to get out of there as soon as possible. If you feel uncomfortable asking people questions in real life the way you imagine they should be asked, chances are you'll feel the same discomfort asking them in a way that's going to help your writing - which may mean you communicate your doubts to the reader more effectively in a scene later on. To develop a voice in dialogue genre as in writing a complete scene, begin with daily utilitarian conversation; learn how to draw the reader into the scene and how to maintain the connection without adding distraction. Keep the pace of the interchanges fitting the context. And then, in dialogue as in real life, there is an urgency to important communication.

As adults, our first memories of dialogue are probably the school plays and pageants in which we starred. These superhero monologues were often given to us by patient, over-achieving parents, whose motivation was partly to help us memorize these grandiloquent utterances and partly to secretly show off how talented their darling little stars really were. If we told you that considering and revising these superhero soliloquies and making them real would be helpful in writing good dialogue, it wouldn't help much because this was then, and dialogue is now. Flash back to when you gave that first performance behind the tilled sheets.

CHAPTER 7

Structuring Your Book

Designing a book with a full outline in mind provides advantages: - Readers can depend on each chapter presenting a fresh idea or thesis about the central topic. - Publishers and editors will like the idea, because they believe readers will gain more satisfaction from a well-organized book. - You will have a checklist to ensure your book covers all the important points. - When you know what comes next in a sequence, writing is easier.

So you have decided that a book could be a great way to share your knowledge and experience with other people. What's next? You need to plan how your book will achieve this. Most good books have a logical structure, or framework, also known as form or plot - not just a random collection of thoughts, as you might find in a collection of essays such as you are reading. It is better to create a clear idea for a book and then focus on writing it. Often, the seed for a book starts with a core idea, to which you add sub-themes in logical sections. These, in turn, comprise individual chapters or discrete sections. Each part of your book builds logically on what has gone before to provide a smoothly integrated whole. If you choose to present your material in a disorganized or random way, it will be harder for readers to understand and digest, and the book will only appeal to a partial or niche audience instead of lots of different types of readers. So let's explore different book structures, and decide how to present the ideas in your book.

6.1. Outlining Your Story

Moreover, your readers won't feel cheated. Plotlines will culminate into meaningful events that shape events or characters and will do so causally and contextually. The audience will be entertained and your talent recognized. As much as writers, directors, and stage programmers push the limits, from Shakespeare to drama theatre, in an effort to adapt life stories, most audiences desire to follow a specific set of characters throughout a series of intelligent and fast-paced actions, culminating in a vivid and satisfying welcome-end, or at least, many significant plot twists. No reader has the time and energy to spend their mostly free-of-charge weekly afternoons and evenings without visible rewards for stepping out of their skins and into a fictional person's mind and heart. It's win-win - a job well done is a job well paid.

As we established, writing a book is a demanding and time-consuming process, with hours of research, development, and writing. A good way to ease this process is to lay the road carefully and in detail, through supporting characters and backstories, the scene and background, plot turns and storyline, pace and tension. Basically, outline your book in a form that you will be able to transform from a list of bullet points into meaningful, nicely written paragraphs of text. This overview initiative will pave the road and provide headache solutions, such as character A that can't be at position Y because he is supposed to be injured and therefore can't jump over a high wall or a heroine that can't be a general in World War II because there were no female generals in that army, etc. This way, the plot will evolve rationally and without unnecessary stress.

CHAPTER 8

The Writing Process

But once you understand the process is consistent and unavoidable, and indeed that feeling lost is its inescapable consequence, then many of these psychological demons evaporate. The writing process is cyclical. At one of the cycles, you're taking an idea and making it work, shoving it, pulling it, intervening, weeping virgin canvas. At another, you're understanding and relating the call which gives coherence to the idea, and to this narrative in which it is suited. These are schizo-creative moments. A preconscious, driven state such when we were struck by first questioning impulse, can coexist with satisfied emergent structuring faculty, and no real discomfort. Then some instinctive feeling, simultaneously compositional and dramatic, combines to jell the story.

A true grasp of the writing process is something that evades many writers. Often, one moment you're heading down fast and easy on the rather congenial path of the opening scenes, then just as suddenly you will find yourself lost in a dark impenetrable forest. The easy thrill of the initial challenge gives way to an oppressive sense of timeslip, and the initial fear and excitement is converted into an unnatural stiffness which can only be dispelled by a strike-out along some distant tangent. The writer finds other things to do, or simply closes the door of their office without daring to enter, chooses any other takers than to write.

7.1. Overcoming Writer's Block

Another way to 'unblock' oneself is to start by writing something irrelevant or totally inappropriate. It doesn't really matter what it is. What matters is only that one writes something. What also works is to write according to a prescribed structure: make a list of topics (say, for a possible future book or autobiography), and 'work through them' without interruption for two hours; or write a 500-word opinion piece, even if you never intend to publish it. Another direction to move in is to change your writing style for half a page, as often as necessary. In other words: write in different ways about unrelated (or only superficially related) topics, one after the other, and notice how the writer's block vanishes without you even noticing it.

To reiterate: I have never suffered from the problem of writer's block. Words are in infinite supply in my head and if ever they dried up, there are plenty of alternatives available to help clear the channels, including going for a walk, taking a bath, playing the piano, or reading a dictionary. But this is not everybody's experience. People often ask me for advice on what to do if words fail and they grind to a halt, unable to write the next word. If my mental dictionary fails, I can always turn to my extra physical dictionaries—or to inspirational books. Get them to open up a fixed number of pages from two or three different dictionaries at random and write down, say, the first ten interesting words defined on each page. Now look at the two or three sets of ten words on your piece of paper and see how they can be connected into some kind of narrative. They might prove to be pointers to a possible direction for your writing.

CHAPTER 9

Editing and Revising

Revisions are considered the most important part of the writer's journey (thinking on paper). The everything-considered final phase other drafts in creating those significant changes that need to be made to make the document even better. To revise, you will evaluate the changes to assess how they would be even more effective in communicating with a reader, to eliminate wordiness by cutting unnecessary words, repetition, and innovating to make your sentences more clear, natural, and precise, to make your paper sound more sophisticated and acceptable in the professional community. This part of the writer's journal is the most important to reach career goals; it isn't easy.

Editing and revising: these two terms are often used interchangeably, yet they carry different connotations. Editing refers to the process of improving the content and quality of a writing piece by adding, removing, and reorganizing words, sentences, or paragraphs. This involves evaluating the relevance of ideas and the logical flow, specificity, and word use. During editing, writers should check their work looking for what should be removed, added, or reorganized. Revisions are the actual changes, a collaboration of solutions to those checks. Editing goes beyond catching typos or incorrect punctuation; it focuses on enhancing the layer of meanings and substantively shaping the nature of the work. Editing and the editor play multiple roles in the process to help the writer achieve career goals from discovery, dualization, artistry, and alignment, the 4 writers' journey mapping criterion to self-discovery to teach how to write the best examples of authoring.

8.1. Self-Editing Techniques

Grammar and spelling checkers: Use these to hunt for initial errors. Bigger errors will shine out like the proverb, and make you embarrassed that such basics could have escaped your attention. Built-in grammar and spell checkers such as the one included in the last few editions of Microsoft Office Word aim to eliminate mistakes that are easy for them to spot. These include wrong word usage, sentence creation errors, inconsistencies in punctuation policies, and many other mid-high end level grammar and spelling issues. You may be uncomfortable with it, but you need tools like this if you expect to have any readers. These aids can make things easier, but make sure you understand the editor's instructions before you accept or ignore them. The grammar and spell-check will help you identify a number of fundamental mistakes, but it leaves a lot of room for mistakes. If necessary, use your editing skills again to ensure maximum individual performance.

Both my publisher and I agree that a writer should pay an editor first before trying to self-edit. His stance is that although I have helped to edit other writers' work in the past, which does cover the point, I do not have the box-office appeal nor the qualifications that justify charging a fee. I also feel and know that I am rubbish at spotting my own errors as many people more qualified than me have pointed out. I also know that many more people who would have done if I had published the book earlier would have been annoyed enough not to read the book to see what I had to say. Therefore anything that helps the writer to spot and repair mistakes has to be a bonus, and here are a few free ones for you to consider.

CHAPTER 10

Seeking Feedback

People have told me that it doesn't bother them at all when a roomful of people yawn while they are giving a speech. It should bother them, but in general, they're not aware of it because they are passionate about what they are presenting. When that isn't a feeling within them, feedback can knock writing way off track. I personally don't live in the hope — usually an illusory one in matters such as this — that if I write something, everyone is going to like it; but I hope that readers get something from my writing that is not a waste of their time.

Whether you have considered the research and prepared a detailed chapter-by-chapter outline or have started writing by the seat of your pants, receiving feedback at this point on your direction is crucial. Go into the arena with your eyes wide open. Expect criticism, both of your writing and the subject of your book. You will have to decide in advance whose input matters — and whose doesn't. Both positive and negative feedback need to be weighed, but this is your book and no one knows your vision better than you do. Indifferent.

9.1. Working with Beta Readers

Beta readers should understand what is expected of them regarding their responsibilities and the turnaround time involved. After setting the expectation, book bloggers can be an excellent source of beta readers. They read widely in their chosen genre and are genuinely interested in helping their favorite authors. Another excellent source of beta readers is author groups, where book swaps take place. I make it a habit to beta read every manuscript I receive, unless it is outside my area of interest, in which case I opt to read an ARC instead. I believe in the concept and it encourages more coherent feedback when I receive my manuscripts. If someone has taken the time to invest in me, I feel an obligation to invest in them. With my second manuscript well on its way, I know that understanding the side of an author will only serve to make me a better beta reader.

The next stage in my journey was to make my story available to "beta" readers. Beta readers are early reviewers who are given a pre-release copy of a book to provide the author with feedback before final editing and publication. Ideally, beta readers will read your book, rather than picking it up and putting it down. They will do more than just cheer you on and tell you how wonderful your book is. They will also provide you with insightful comments that add value and assist with your second or third draft. While I believe that I had a strong manuscript, it definitely benefited from feedback given by my beta readers. In fact, I had many of the errors and inconsistencies that I learned to look out for as a beta reader when it came time to read an ARC (advanced review copy) of someone else's manuscript.

CHAPTER 11

Preparing for Publication

Step 5: Remind the agent that he or she works for you, the personal project, so the agent should always reach out and seek clarity if the author does not explicitly understand. Have clarity about the division of roles and communication format before a title is signed. The "I'm too busy to explain" line is not acceptable. If the agent has time to meet up with friends, spend fun time with family, or grab dinner at a swanky restaurant, then he or she has a chance to prioritize a mutually beneficial conversation. The more the author knows, the more informed the decision.

Step 4: Don't sign anything in haste out of fear, scarcity, or greed. The agent works for the author, who should judiciously weigh the pros and cons of every decision. If an author feels a time crunch to sign a publishing contract, ask for an extension before signing anything that isn't absolutely understood and agreed upon.

Step 1: Read the contract before you sign it. Ask for a two-year "out" clause if, after a year or two, your agent hasn't been able to place the book with a publisher. How much money is required to break the contract, and what are the "kill fees" (such as paying back the money the agent has already spent submitting your proposal to publishers) if you do need to sever the relationship early? Sometimes an agent isn't the right match or indeed is too new to find you a publisher.

Timing: Accepting an agent's offer for your book often just means that the sale will happen anytime during the next year. Acquisition is continuous, with agents typically pitching the next big title to assistant editors, senior editors, or publishers each week.

The basics: First, you'll need an agent (unless you have a lawyer in the family able to do the negotiations), so research various agents online or by visiting your favorite bookstore. A book published after being submitted by an agent is much more likely to be carried by bookstores because those publishers have a reputation for quality and reliability. Be sure to follow the submission guidelines for each particular agent as well as possible; they'll appreciate the effort.

10.1. Understanding Publishing Options

This section covers choosing a publisher, working with an agent, and promotes selecting the best publishing option. Explore the publishing options to learn what publishing path would be best for your work. There are four key methods to have your written novel in the hands of a reader. Each of the previous options would allow you to write the novel you want to share with the world.

Avoid some of the mistakes ahead of time, including creating competitive analysis and research documents so you understand your market and your competition. Evaluate each venue for your book based on the best fit for your goals. There is no single path to getting a book on the shelves. Only your passion should make you want to invest hundreds of hours and probably thousands of dollars to wade through the publishing landscape.

Self-publishing allows authors to write for less mainstream markets and avoid political and religious topics. They also have greater quality control and faster publication than traditional markets and can find a quicker market for their work.

Traditional publishers typically contract professional editors, proofreaders, and reviewers to improve the writing and the story. They utilize widely recognized processes to go from an idea to a finished book product, targeting niche markets with various distribution channels. Often, there are complex contracts in place compensating key players based on the performance of the published work. The books they publish are also found on the shelves at bookstores and libraries.

CHAPTER 12

Marketing and Promoting Your Book

There are many other ways to promote your book, both before and after it comes out. Premature promotion is expensive so decide if it's worthwhile. While I try to save a little here and there as part of my site's promotion budget, costs add up quickly after the book has been published. However you do it, whatever financial route you choose, remember not to stop publicizing your book. The more people who know about your book, the better the chances are that it will sell. But I can't end this section without a piece of advice that I believe is a really important part of a writer's job—it's up to you to create the buzz the book needs, because you aren't just an author. You're your best friend and publicist, too. Good luck!

When I knew that Let Me Die In His Footsteps was almost ready, I researched websites to advertise my book. I can't afford to pay for a huge ad in the New York Times, but I sure can place an ad on the New York Times website that will showcase my book for a Sunday, which traditionally has been known as book ad day. Years ago, when I lived in Los Angeles I'd taken ads on the L.A. Times website—I knew how much those ads drove traffic to my site. Now that I live in Kentucky and couldn't afford L.A. Times prices, I checked with Lexington's hometown Star. Right up front, I'm going to confess I was disappointed in the Star's numbers, visible on their front page. When I dialed the number to do my buy, I asked the young salesperson about those numbers. It was explained to me that the huge difference in numbers occurred because the NY Times has so many more readers than the Lexington Star. Logical, when you think about it.

Once your novel sees the light of day, your work has only just begun. Marketing your book can be daunting and overwhelming. Here are a few basic steps you can take to give your book the best possible chances for commercial and critical success.

11.1. Building an Author Platform

The word of mouth method of marketing spreads around to outdo any other method. You've probably scrolled through Amazon or another method of shopping and bought a book because a friend or family member told you that it was the best book they'd ever read. All of us have. That's what we're after—a buzz. The methods of creating buzz can be big or small. There are the traditional social media methods of Facebook, Twitter, Pinterest, Snapchat, and even YouTube. Each author out there has a different combination of platforms that they feel comfortable with. Some like Goodreads while others cringe dealing with it. There are actual sales going on at LinkedIn. The field has grown. You don't have to break your bank account either because for every upcharge, you have twice as many free things you can do. The best part about developing an author platform is creating relationships with other people. You don't make friends to sell books. You make friends because you like them. And if you really like them, you just might promote their work to your own friends. I get it. Some folks are smarter than me, and they'll blast email their list twice a day between Twitter posts every three minutes. That's fine. It never hurts to remember that actual interactions are happening behind those screens of social media.

What is an author platform and do you need one to become published? Simple answer: Yes! If you want to sell books. As I said in my introduction, the world changed when ebooks hit the market and nothing has changed the world of publishing as much as the advent of self-publishing. Still, writing great books is only one part of selling books. You need a way to be seen. The best part is you have the freedom to build it your way. The algorithms are complicated, but it all begins with someone somewhere talking about your book.

CHAPTER 13

Navigating the Publishing Industry

I also learned that a little basic knowledge of how the book production process works – from manuscript to printed book – would have been very helpful. There are standards, conventions, and scribal traditions you need to know if you want to talk to book professionals in a way that frees you to use your creativity to best advantage. I discovered that a little learning doesn't just reduce potential misunderstandings but makes the conversation richer and more interesting for both parties.

I discovered that, although some rules govern how the publishing industry works, the personalities, pressures, and priorities of individual people, including agents, editors, and writers, are also very much part of this landscape I sought to enter. Understanding a little about what motivates each of these players, and how they often regard each other, can go a long way towards finding your own way through this complex and ever-changing world.

12.1. Understanding Literary Agents

Sure, sometimes an agent may turn down a manuscript for personal reasons or choose not to pursue a project because it's not a good fit, but most work is rejected because it's not ready, not because it's not worth representing if the author is willing to put the time in to improve on it.

So who the heck are these mysterious literary agents, and how do you go about getting one of them to take you on? A literary agent works with both the author and the publisher to sell books and represent an author's interests. They will typically sit down with a potential author to discuss their work and advise if any work is needed before the agent can represent you effectively and negotiate a good deal on your behalf. It's important to remember that if a project is rejected, it's because it's probably not a good business deal - agents make money by negotiating the best possible deals for their clients. If they can't do this, then neither party makes any money.

CHAPTER 14

Self-Publishing vs. Traditional Publishing

Self-publishing very much favors non-fiction over fiction. Non-fiction books don't need hefty promotion budgets. Whether they are history, biography, memoir, or a subject fewer writers than readers want to know more about, their success depends more on long-term word-of-mouth than on a hyperactive launch. Non-fiction writers have to be prepared to promote their books indefinitely, and to keep the content relevant.

Self-publishing This is an increasingly popular way to bring a book to people's attention and be remunerated for it. Over five million self-published books are available on Amazon, and if writers want to keep control of their rights, earn higher royalties, and see their books published far more swiftly than they would receive an advance from a commercial publisher, this is the way for them.

There's a world of difference between self-publishing and traditional (a.k.a. commercial or trade) publishing. As their suffixes imply, in traditional publishing, the publisher does everything. It pays for the book to be produced, distributed, marketed, and sold, and above all, it makes the decisions. With self-publishing, the writer does all these things, and has the say about the decisions. The writer can also choose whether to employ helpers, such as a freelance copy-editor or proofreader, designer, or marketing expert.

13.1. *Pros and Cons of Each Path*

Most writers go through a period of wanting to be traditionally published and hoping that their stories will find a home there. Then quite a few accept that they'll probably be self-publishing and write stories for themselves. Perhaps to share with a tiny circle of friends, about whom many cautionary tales use the words "grateful for" or "know a lot of", or because the stories that pour out of you because you have to write them aren't marketable. Or to experiment with the form, focus on a particular style, or prove something to themselves.

Self-publishing can be extremely rewarding, and an increasing number of writers are taking this route. But it's neither easier nor quicker than the traditional route, and its rewards of much higher royalties for each copy sold come with the need for money to print, put it out there, and create, hire, or outsource tasks that the traditional publisher would normally take care of. This section discusses the pros and cons of each path, assuming that your book has a good cover and is well edited and formatted. Just because you can bypass the traditional route by self-publishing doesn't mean that you should. Nor do the choices have to be exclusive. Your book(s) are always available virtually forever, one way or another. Bookstores can want a title "in anticipation" of its arrival.

CHAPTER 15

Legal and Copyright Considerations

From the author's point of view, once the work leaves her computer or isn't under her direct control, in theory it is out of her control, too. Frankly, very few authors pay attention to copyright control per se, in that the author's only recourse for stopping illegal use of her work, or for collecting money from its commission, is through civil law, a situation that generally precludes litigation unless the financial rewards are potentially lucrative. Although it's the graphics that are key as to obtaining permissions, don't assume that music and out-of-print books and journals are free to use. Even noncommercial or educational use may require permission and payment.

When you publish a book, for practical or businesslike reasons, you should consider certain facets. First, copyright laws are designed (in theory) to protect creative works by allowing the copyright owner to exclusively profit from and control the work. The copyright owner is usually the author, though the author can transfer the copyright (although most book contracts make this specific) to someone else. When copyright is not specifically transferred by contract to a publisher, most publishers will not publish your book. Reproduction of another's copyrighted work without permission is a big no-no and is likely to lead to legal action.

14.1. Protecting Your Intellectual Property

The copyright law is a creature of the United States Congress. It is not honored around the world except as adopted in international conventions. However, during the last few years the United States has been negotiating with other countries to continue some 40 separate bilateral agreements into a general multilateral agreement that would protect greater rights of the literary creator.

Producing a book is such a considerable undertaking, and so much is at stake, that it behooves the writer to take precautionary steps to keep the copyright from being infringed upon. Copyright to one's writing is automatic, but the completed form of the book is not. As you write your book, it is important that you mark the manuscript with a copyright symbol, C within a circle - © - followed by your name and the year. This is a constant reminder to potential infringers that what they are reading has a legal owner. In addition, it is important that if you copy sections, either of your book or from a published writing, that these materials are returned to your locked file cabinet immediately.

CHAPTER 16

Building a Writing Routine

The important thing is that you put words on the page regularly, even if it's only one sentence a day. The only way to write a book is one word at a time, so each day, write something that will bring you and your book closer together. To refine your routine, take into account the time of day you work best as well as your working circumstances. Make sure that your routine is regularly discussed with your spouse/partner when you live together, so that household problems don't unnecessarily interfere with the time spent writing. Establish rules for the lifestyle you are both willing to lead to accommodate a book project. You might, for example, agree on a writing schedule, vacations, or shared chores.

Setting up a writing routine that allows you to put words on the page regularly is as individual as writing itself. Every writer has a different process and therefore different needs. Through a lot of trial and error, I eventually found a routine that works for me. It allows me to write even when I'm busy and restless and have more writing time than I know what to do with. With a little bit of ingenuity and a great deal of understanding and support from my husband, I've also written books under less than ideal circumstances, while traveling and even with three children at home. It's all a matter of creating a routine that's uniquely yours and safeguarding the time and energy you need to write. Remember, though, that a writing routine has to come to life, grow, and change with you. Be flexible to experiment with different parts of the routine if one piece or another stops working for you.

15.1. Finding Your Ideal Writing Schedule

Working on research papers, business reports, or several-thousand-word essays has given you at least a vague idea of what it took to write your story work. However, technology now makes the task simpler because you can store your book project electronically, or you can write in the same way that you use your e-mail or word-processing program. Your time planning and your organizational skills are still important, and it can be helpful to have a plan before you even start. Since many novel writers cannot go back and alter anything on paper, it's vital to have a distinct impression of the story you're over and not lose your place.

We would all love to have the luxury of uninterrupted writing time and sequester ourselves in a garret for days on end. But life's constraints are a very real part of being a professional writer. To successfully work around a rigorous school schedule, full-time job, or other responsibilities, adopt time management strategies and incorporate them into a system that works. By learning to write in short bursts or during off-peak hours, it is possible to fit book writing around life's other obligations.

CHAPTER 17

Balancing Writing with Other Commitments

All writers, whatever your more mundane commitments, will have that manuscript niggling at them during their work time. That doesn't make you any different from other professional writers with different eight-hour-a-day occupations to worry about. Group them together in your mind and work on each separately. When you're at work, work. When you're writing, write. Whatever happens, insist on yourself that, no matter what, you're not going to fail in being in one frame of mind for the other profession and vice versa.

The most important lesson you must learn is that you will fail to get the balance right more often than not. That goes without saying, and you should just accept that it will happen. The real balancing act is in those moments when you do have to take a seat at your desk amidst the chaos. You have to be efficient, very thorough, and clear in your planning and management of time. This will enable you to make the most out of what little time you have in front of the computer.

16.1. Time Management Strategies

Using a timer is what helped my writer's time management more than anything else. I'd set the timer for, say, only fifteen minutes. Writing was not the only activity I "wrote" on my schedule. I also had time for planning my activities, for relaxation, for everyday chores. I found that a short time of commitment to writing freed me from the feeling of being overwhelmed and from physical pain as well. I'd plan to write often during a day with time for other activities between. When I looked at what I'd written, I was pleased, and when I thought about writing again, I wanted to continue.

As a full-time teacher with only about an hour of time each school day to write during my first summer break, I learned that writing from midnight to 3:00 to meet deadlines set for myself was not helpful, but I often found myself writing then. All stories work together in a writer's mind and demand to be put on paper first. The use of a timer with another activity for a short time is the best way to meet a writer's write/other activities balance and manage time effectively. Writing is never forced, so writing will be enjoyable. Also, deadlines, which do serve the wise writer, will not have to be made by midnight or dawn but within reason.

The following is an excerpt from the book "How to Write a Book: From Vision to Bookshelf" by Vivian Zabel.

CHAPTER 18

Staying Motivated and Focused

Too many writers hold onto their work too long and are afraid to share it with the world. If you find yourself endlessly writing and rewriting, it's probably time to let other people see your manuscript. A common factor that slows writers down is not a lack of motivation, but a lack of courage. Can you relate to any of these sentiments? "I'm going to let my friend read it when it's finished." "Once my revisions are complete, I'll see if the editor likes it." "I'm scared to send it out." "I'm dying to see what people think, but everyone says it's dull and predictable." If you trust the talent and judgment of your literary friends who encourage you to show your work, give them the benefit of the doubt. Don't forget to take breaks! Regular rest periods are essential for all writers, particularly those suffering from overuse injuries such as carpal tunnel syndrome and writer's cramp. Relaxation and healing can come in many forms.

Writing involves many different aspects - editing, typing, researching, promoting, packaging, not to mention the writing itself. Not only that, but in many instances, writing is a solitary adventure. It's just you and your computer. Some authors struggle with feelings of insecurity and failure. Booking public readings, doing author signings, providing review copies, going on a promotional tour - these public appearances can instill stress, exacerbate feelings of anxiety and inadequacy, and take away from valuable writing time. Just like getting to the gym, sometimes motivating yourself to write is a challenge, but it's important to stay the course and continually persist in trying to achieve your goals.

17.1. Setting Achievable Writing Goals

Most problem-solving books on writing could be summed up as "find a method that works for you". Many don't really tackle the theory of creativity - but that's the central aim of Breaking the Writer's Block: the psychology of the process. At its most basic level, creativity is a process that moves on whether you like it or not. I found inescapable staircases eerily helpful as a metaphor for this. The passage of time can make arts of the mundane and mechanical sides of creativity, if done properly, and with a certain structured leniency towards yourself.

Great ideas are one thing, but when writing a book, especially a full-length novel, inspiration and creativity might not be enough to keep you going until the very end. Sure, they're essential ingredients. However, to bring your creative project to fruition, you'll need those tried-and-true, nuts-and-bolts workhorses - determination, hard plain work, perseverance, and setting achievable writing goals. So get a reality check on your writing habits before you start because you might have to change them as part of becoming a better, more efficient writer. After all, if you can't establish the writing practice you started in Module One, then creating something as complex as a full-length novel will be doubly difficult. This is where other writers' collected wisdom can help.

CHAPTER 19

The Importance of Community

Getting my book published has turned out to be less of a struggle than creating a product that stands on its own. The enormous enthusiasm and shared efforts have invigorated me, with contributions from the professionals at Repeater Books – like Sallyanne, who has an unbridled passion, Clare Robertson, who has a sharp-editing eye, and co-directors, Tamar Shlaim and Mark Fisher – book friend Lesley Speed, who commented and made final edits for many of the significant illustrations, and my immediate family and friends, including Toby Pennington and Karen and John Fiennes, who reviewed multiple edits and the whole submission package. Engaging so many people is testament to the unifying power of building from shared interest. To be a successful writer or to achieve anything more abstract, the importance of community, shared values yet diverse pursuits, rank above the individual sacrifice. At crucial times in almost everything I have done, this has been the great constant. My community gives me the muscle, strength and voice, and I need these things when I am lost in my head, wandering distant thought paths, which can be distracting, happy, touching, but always lonely and far less purposeful without diverse others who quickly bring me down to earth.

At the best of times, writing a book is a solitary endeavor. Along with sheer hard, consistent work and an ability to communicate in a dynamic way to capture interest, the magical, mysterious process follows a particular path. Its end result is a finished story and the exciting, emotionally rewarding ability to share it with an audience, to finally transform that solitary inclination into a meaningful engagement with others. I've always believed that a book needs to live on its own, in its own world, speaking in the reader's voice to be molded by the individual, separate and unique from the creator. The creator's intention is irrelevant once the reader has begun. It always somehow makes me sad and a little bit angry when an author states that their work is beyond interpretation. A book is a dialogue between the creator and the reader. It has its own spirit, independent, volatile, ever inviting interpretation, waiting to be breathed to life by the reader. The author is the midwife only. Once the book is in the air, delivery complete, its secrets become the reader's to revel in.

18.1. Joining Writing Groups

It's important to connect with others who are on the same journey. There's so much to learn from each other. Like attracts like, so in your pursuit of writing and publishing, you will begin to meet others with similar interests. This doesn't only mean that you will make friends with aspiring writers; you may also come in contact or become friends with already-established and seasoned authors. It would be in your interest to make friends and expand your network. Indeed, these connections might open doors for character cameos and book signings. In addition to attending literary events, you may want to take a writing class at a local college or support a writing group, which will help to improve your skills over time and keep you committed to finishing your book. Also, writing partners, also known as writing friends, can serve as a valuable tool on your journey. You can seek consumer feedback on your work from your colleagues. Also, frequenting the local library or campsite may also give you the opportunity to meet with publishing insiders who can provide assistance in your endeavors.

CHAPTER 20

Celebrating Milestones

Make a big deal out of getting an agent, a publishing agreement, or a query returned with interest. Definitely celebrate each award nomination, and winning generates the need for a huge dinner. Going to a book launch is a great way to congratulate an author friend, and it gives you a chance to pick up some tips for your own book. If you and your friend are both writers, see about writing your own short story or novel anthology. Use these milestones as a reason to acknowledge the determination of your colleagues and to help maintain your commitment.

When someone in your writing group finishes the first draft, celebrate! Bring something special to drink or give her some flowers. Sharing a toast to a six-month goal met with well-crafted writing is rewarding and energizing. Celebrate when the edits are finished. Bring flowers, chocolate, or a bottle of wine to share as you acknowledge the fruits of labor. These gestures may seem small, but they are important. Each of those drafts takes time and is testimony to the discipline and determination to move forward. Energize and acknowledge your advancements by hearing others discuss your work.

It does not take away from the dedication each person put into their part, but it does build stronger scar tissue.

19.1. Acknowledging Your Achievements

You have taken this course to be a better writer and have probably raised doubts about your ability to write. You can let go of these concerns now. You have succeeded in your ambition. You have written a book. It will be a better book than most aspiring writers set out to create because you did the work needed to write the book you wanted to write and didn't simply leave it as a pondered dream. When this course offered you the question of learning another module or to continue with writing that novel, brokering permission from our tutors, it was always "Is this what you really want to do? Follow your dream!" That is a monumental claim, one which could be met repeatedly because it is important: The whole course is about Dreaming Big and Definitely Doing. Once those decisions have been made, it is only a short step to producing a book.

Throughout this course, I have set countless writing tasks designed to test your stamina as a writer, sparked your imagination, and helped you to explore ideas, to define the main themes, and recognize the individual journey these give. During that time, you have worked diligently, writing thousands of words in anticipation of producing a polished piece of work. Dedication and hard work are commendable and should never be underestimated. Yet how often have you paused to congratulate yourself? It often feels as if we are "just doing our job" when we achieve these things and forget to acknowledge the significance of our achievements. Let me assert that, in doing what you have done so far in this course, and by taking the initiative to learn in general, you have achieved something momentous. It takes grit and determination to accomplish your training schedule, and more to do the course required to earn your degree or diploma. It seems we are left with a gulf in achievement.

What would happen were we to recognize that while the step of earning a degree is a considerable one, taking the course, and undertaking the study, is a considerable accomplishment as well?

CHAPTER 21

Overcoming Rejection and Criticism

You can also build your own network now through multiple avenues by promoting your work on your website, with press releases, on sites like Authors Den, Facebook, Twitter, or linking to similar blogs and sites. It is important to network. I also recommend that you do quite a bit of research to discover which agents or publishers represent what and what kinds of contracts other writers are offered. If you know who you are submitting to as well as you know your own writing, it is much easier to write a good prologue or query letter, explore publishing support from various industry professionals, pantster or plotter? StringBuilder allows you to discover and develop your core narrative strategy. If you intended to query agents or publishers as well, contact information for more than one hundred agents and much more detailed information to end the ending on your terms. Your readers will thank you.

All writers face rejection, even famous and successful ones. It is important to remember that it is not a personal attack but merely someone saying no to your product. Tenacity is a writer's most powerful tool. The reality is that not everyone is going to get our writing, but others will. Look for the others who like what you do and keep building on that. When an agent or publisher recognizes your genius and offers you a contract, it is your chance to be selective also. Make sure your work fits with what they are offering, what you want, and build a lasting, valuable relationship in your corner for your entire career. You need someone who will not only represent your work, but who also has and shares your vision for the long term. Don't be surprised if the process takes time.

20.1. Developing Resilience

The more resilient you become, the more unassailable your work. At some point, most of you will have read something or saw something that was terrible – truly awful – and still went on to be a success. However, without resilience, this can be difficult to truly comprehend. If you are able to view criticism as subjective opinion, then a "no" becomes little more than relevance to the moment – what might be bad at one point in time might resonate at another. Refusing to accept failure will mean you will take those negative comments and just keep on going, instead of internalizing them as the truth. And finally, once your work is out there, you need to have resilience like adamant – especially if doing the promotional work yourself. Folk who don't like writer's message can be the most cruel. But remember – they have nothing on those – like you – who have continued to follow their dreams.

Resilience is both a trait and a skill – it is both about who we are and how we manage our situations. As a writer, learning to develop resilience is the key to survival. There will be rejections, there will be knock-backs, there will be negative reviews, there will be criticisms, and sometimes there will even be that long, barren desert your creativity gets lost in. But to consider failure as an option actually makes it an option. If a writer truly loves to write, then giving up isn't a question. Instead, use those negatives to fuel your desire to improve. And refuse to let a "no" be the end. It is only someone else's opinion. If your writing passion is sincere enough, it will also be infectious to others at some time.

CHAPTER 22

The Writer's Mindset

The term "writer's mindset" refers not just to the writer's readiness to write, but also to underlying and enabling aspects of your mental formation that will nourish your writing and give it backbone. Just as an architect always works upon a foundation and with the perspective of a multi-story building in mind, so, too, should a writer take care in the development of particular baselines and perspectives that are fundamental to their future creative writing success.

It is often tempting to think that if you have the creativity and skills to write, a book will automatically result - but the actual process of writing any work, whether or not it ends up in book form, is neither automatic nor instantaneous. You should start out with reasonable expectations as to how your writing process may evolve - realizing it is a learning experience and making allowances for that fact, and pacing yourself and your work accordingly.

21.1. Cultivating a Growth Mindset

A growth mindset is the foundation of all success, be it writing or anything else. It's the recognition that with effort, we can improve our abilities and with time, trust me, we do. Every day, I tell myself that I'm a more competent writer than I was yesterday. And it's true. Not because I simply tell myself that, but because I try new methods and strategies, I study the work of other authors, and I make time for writing each day. A perfectionist would shy away and believe that any mistakes (a.k.a learning points) will call for overt indignation about their own being, but a growth-minded person sees trials and tribulations as... well, as part of the process. To become growth-minded writers, we choose how we respond to our circumstances. We can resist and spend energy on placing blame on others, or we can accept that we're not perfect and that it's okay. Then we can learn what we need to know in order to be more equipped for the future.

Usually, when a writer talks about learning and self-improvement, they're talking about how to improve your writing. But the truth is, before any of those other writing tips can be put into action, a writer must first cultivate a growth mindset in their writing and themselves. Our beliefs about our abilities bring up other hindrances. If we believe our abilities are essentially unchanging, we deal a massive hindrance to our efforts. You may say to yourself, "I'm not that good at X, but I'm really good at Y." This is known as a fixed mindset. Because you believe it's impossible to improve, you don't try to develop your competency, and from there, confidence. If someone sneers and tells you that you might as well quit trying, deep down, you already believe it. For example, you may feel like you're not a "math person," and that no amount of effort could ever change that. But, with a growth mindset, you would recognize your limitations and put more effort into it because you recognize that the only way is up.

CHAPTER 23

Writing Across Genres

In the top half of the cozy Writing And Reading fire pit we call Baylor House, I rekindled a passion for fiction and a deep desire to know what Texas writers have to say. I witnessed my concentration multiply and multiply again. This essay is "The House I Am Running From" by Nancy Hutchins. As Nancy'll tell you a few pages on, reading, even writing, across genres encompasses discoveries humility encourages. Readers of any genre can learn a great deal about themselves and their writing. With this curiosity intact, I soon realized the number of pieces could serve long-term as book chapters, sewing the genres together.

In 1999, I embarked on a yearlong journey through poetry, fiction, and creative nonfiction aimed at examining the borders drawn between one genre and another. I theorized before the year began, and have come to believe even more deeply since its end, that all literary art strives toward the same goals. That the same sentence can be, in some small way, both Stanley Plumly's and Raymond Chandler's. That convergence helps readers break down barriers separating one genre from another and ultimately allowing us to appreciate each genre better.

22.1. Experimenting with Different Styles

The desired result is gaining forthrightness, the ability to hold the narrative voice and the flow of character movements or thoughts. It is of paramount importance that you should not only connect to the story but also become the storyteller. Recall the famous 'The Theory of Relativity' and write down the entire story so that its effect is the same as what had occurred. Shortlist the accomplished results. This exercise accomplishes more than just familiarizing you with various styles in the market. The curiosity and doubt piqued by the way a particular paragraph transitions into the next gets covered here itself. After writing a few paragraphs using this method, you would have understood which style you have been successful in making the story sound like using the bestseller approach. A rare and classic find would impact not only the narrative, characters, or scene, but also the diction and the metaphoric skills. You would know the path you are required to adopt, or traverse, to achieve the same effect.

If you are unsure about how to go about writing and want to experiment by incorporating someone else's style, here is a unique way to go about it while you tread your writer's voyage. Open any random book, preferably a bestseller or a classic, and choose a paragraph that interests you. Once done, type it, making sure that there is no variation in the text you typed, and save it in a new file. If you are computer savvy and keen on technology, you could also use the 'notepad' or 'memo' function on your smartphone. After completing this task, write the next paragraph using this paragraph as an already written starting point. At any given time if inspiration eludes you, seek it by repeating this process.

Writing your book will be a separate experience in itself. Writing becomes easy and what you pen down becomes exciting if the narrative reflects your inner self. To reach that stage, it is important to experiment with different styles in the start. You would have read various genres and styles of writing by several authors. However, developing your style of writing, a style that is distinct, is a different game.

CHAPTER 24

The Future of Publishing

Writing for the audience, however defined, is it. If everyone is the market – is his reader the consumer? It jarred that sharing stories was even considered by one panel member to be a valid motivation for a storyline. If Reading Retreat participants are transitioning from consumers of a book to actually doing the very hard work involved in actually being a writer then readers as consumers are the people who feed a market who in turn support an industry. The link between readers high up on Everest steeper slopes and the authors and their friends and family members seems intact. Long digressions at a panel on potential stories not only showed that these non-professional wordsmiths could multi-plot but actually felt most comfortable plotting together.

Books in audio have come from a studio recording and a strict contract signed between reader and a medium that entailed a time commitment that diminished with the removal of a CD manufacturing process. MP3 files enabled individual delivery via the net and a personal player. Market possibilities have opened up, including downloaded briefings and novellas, the best of radio, talks and performance therefore expected into podcasts. Recording artists will potentially be able to lend support and promote titles in a manner more digitally demanded. Internet cafe culture for spreads via social networking and video site connections set up in-store listening posts that everyone short of the overcautious accept in music retailing. Both landscape and portrait still fit. It's easy for advertisers and sponsor-driven promotions. The Holy Grail still only glimmers.

As a consequence of the Reading Retreat, digital output is available in Amazon's e-books on their new Kindle and the Sony Reader and available to download onto the netbook or iPhone. It is not just Amazon listing a selection of books at cheaper prices, readers are buying them, downloading them, and starting to read them. There is potential for them reading them, finishing them, recommending them or not to others. Metadata may determinedly try to nest writers into particular sales valleys but the reality is that digital is skyscraping. Output into audio books has been largely confined to work from authors already selling extremely well. An umbrella harboring those who have slipped into the mid-list is so far not in the hands of publishers.

No one knows the future. Partners don't. Children don't. Publishers or literary agents or writers don't. But many are hopeful or concerned. There are a host of different potential outcomes. This is an industry during upheaval. Business plans can be revised or rejected, the reader is king. A customer is an individual who, if let down or unsatisfied with their last reading experience they pay for, may never walk into a Waterstones again. The slew of electronic books that have been bought and not finished watching the hundreds of TV channels available 24-hours a day without viewers having to go out to a cinema or video store that could be competing with reading a piece of paper-infrastructure, food or drink that may be selected over a book and commitment to it is growing.

23.1. Emerging Trends and Technologies

23.3 Academic Karma Are you enthusiastic about scholarly communication? Academic Karma advocates for transparency, reproducibility, equality, and distribution. Their mission is to democratize the academic review process, enabling academics to control how and where their work is reviewed and valued and to share the peer review system.

23.2 ShareYourPaper ShareYourPaper is an open-source paper repository aiming to make scholarship accessible to everyone by enabling SSH researchers to share their articles and get support during the depositing process. Researchers around the world can upload and share their work, receive references to articles that are often behind paywalls, create bibliographies for publication, and find other relevant papers for their research.

23.1 LearnSciJournals Imagine a YouTube for educators. LearnSciJournals uses videos, podcasts, and traditional PDF articles to help microbiology researchers engage with primary science to tangibly improve lab courses. They provide other educational resources and activities related to some of the papers, such as lab question guides and group discussions. Their mission is to democratize distance education and make both research and educational resources more discoverable, better engaged with, understood, and utilized.

Introduction The development of Web 2.0 and the wide variety of services enabled by the web for content creation, sharing, and searching have affected individuals' lives in many ways. For scholarly publishing, the process of identifying, synthesizing, and discussing scholarly content had remained fundamentally unchanged over the centuries, with researchers writing papers and publishers producing journals. In the past few years, various platforms have built a reputation for conducting the peer review process and potentially slimming down costs. However, the overwhelming majority of scholarly work continues to be published through the established and highly reputable journals.

CHAPTER 25

Conclusion and Final Thoughts

In the second part of this book, we have taken the process of writing a book through a series of detailed steps, each of which gives you some practical strategies. These practical strategies are designed to help you complete all the tasks needed to go from a blank page to a book ready for the publisher. We have offered 59 "how to" strategies, including how to find the time to write. These are supplemented with the more detailed explanations found in Stepville and In Depth. This part of the book, however, is directed at practical tasks such as organizing your research, writing chapters, and developing an index. Some steps, such as feeding back your manuscript to get it reviewed, should be tried later. That said, if you find that the Stepville steps multiplied like Gremlins, then you may have a rather large book at your table.

In the first part of this book, we asked whether you have it in you to write a book. We explored this question by answering a series of questions covering topics as varied as what kind of person you are, the nature of your ambition, what you want the book to do, and how you view books, readers, ignorance, and knowledge. In doing so, we wrote about the fears and doubts that often frame people's ambitions to write. We also touched on your reasons for wanting your book on the shelf - or on the web. In short, we asked what makes your ambition to write so strong that you are willing to go through the long hours and frequent disappointments of writing a book. If you have answered yes to taking this journey, then we may have left you with some tools for getting started, as well as buttressing your determination to pursue your ambition. As such, the answer is that therefore you can write a book.

24.1. Reflecting on Your Writing Journey

At the end of your book and having satiated the journey from beginning to end, asking the question of yourself, "where do I go from here?" is a healthy question. It demonstrates growth has occurred. You've traveled from point A to point B. Allow yourself a moment to figuratively lift the weight from your legs, sit down and figuratively breathe. Then reset your marker and move forward.

Writing a book is a journey. Discoveries are made. Lamentations are heard. There is joy, sadness, hopes. There are triumphs and failures, and sometimes, all of these occur within the same chapter. A manuscript has a beginning, a middle, and an end. And each of these contributes to your personal growth as a writer.

Toward the end of a book, after writing and polishing everything, I find myself adrift. I begin to wonder what I'm going to write next. Having my mind already moving forward with other ideas upsets me. Yet just the opposite reaction often comes upon finishing, which is, thinking that everything written is worthless. Neither is worthy because it is all a part of the journey.

CHAPTER 26

Publishing Links to help you with your books

Here are some great options for creating fantastic covers:
Economy Covers: https://tinyurl.com/5mhubyby
Premium Covers: https://tinyurl.com/yt3daf87
Here are some great options for Book Editing:
Premium: https://shorturl.at/tqdAz
Here are some great options for Book formatting:
Economy: https://shorturl.at/jNvsu
Here is a great master your audiobook to acx and audible requirements
https://tinyurl.com/ye2xkmna